MOPHEAD

For those who stick out

MOPHEAD

How Your Difference Makes a Difference

by Selina Tusitala Marsh

She drew me too!

AUCKLAND
UNIVERSITY
PRESS

When I was 10
I was teased for having

hair.

Not just thick curly hair

BUT

wild

Afakasi

hair.

Afakasi = being Samoan
+ something else.

I got **thick**

Wavy hair

from my

Samoan

Tuvaluan
mum,

thin and curly

hair from my

New Zealand → Our house

Scottish →

English ←

French dad. →

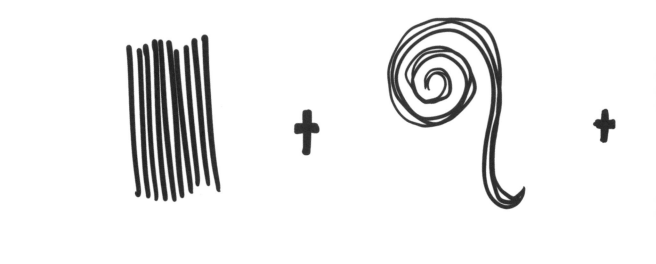

+

+

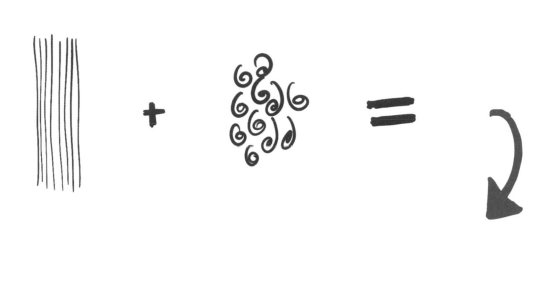

gravity

defied

it

wild

so

was

hair

My

and didn't come back down to earth.

So big it wouldn't fit under hats

or caps.

It broke the cute bows
and clips other girls wore.
Kids called me ...

I was tall, skinny and brown
like the mop in our garage.

It smelled like old socks.

The mop had a head made from hundreds of cotton threads and a long body made of wood.

Being called Mophead
made me feel bad.

I tried to ignore the teasing
but it just got louder.

I cut it.

Some kids
called me

Fuzzy-Wuzzy!

Golliwog!

I wore it in plaits like
Pippi Longstocking.

Some kids
called me

Pippi **Black**stocking!

So I tied it back in a tight bun.
No one called me anything then.

I was the

same.

But we're not made
to be the same.

At home I'd let my
hair out and be ...

a champion rider,

Go
Black Beauty!

a chart-topping singer,

But at school it was a different story.

Then one day a famous poet visited our school.

He
was
tall
and
thin.

They know the way a

He had **WILD** hair

mountain laughs

and **WILD** words.

Sam was not the same.
He loved being different.

School Policy on Stickmen

It's said that children should not use stick figures when they draw and yet...

We were the same kind of

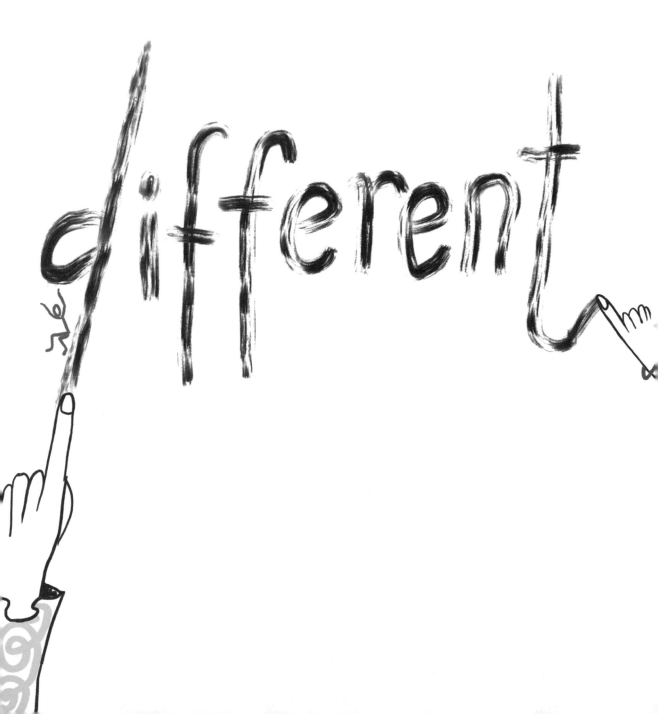

That's when
I decided I
WOULDN'T
be

tied

BACK.

I

WAS

GOING

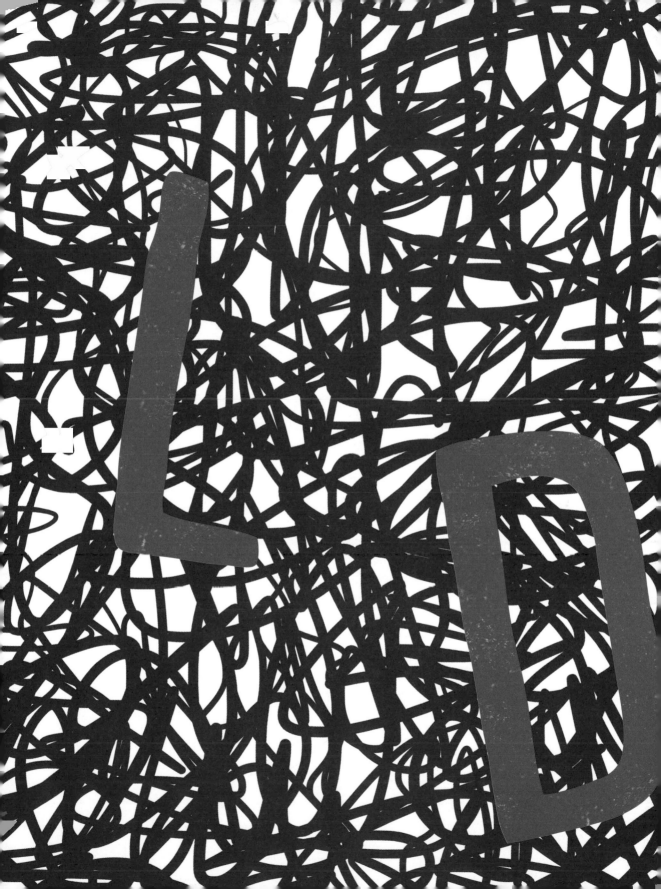

I wore my hair **WILD** at high school.

I wore it **WILD** at university.

I searched for other WILD women.

I discovered the WILD words of Pacific Island women poets.

Konai
TONGA

Momoe
SAMOA

Jully
SOLOMON ISLANDS

Grace
VANUATU

Haunani-Kay
HAWAI'I

I wish I'd met these poets
when I was at school.

Maybe others still could,

so I wrote a PhD thesis on them.

I wrote lots about their poetry and wondered ...

could I do that?

And the award for
Best First Book is ...

fast talking PI
by Selina Tusitala Marsh.

People liked my words

and invited me to do cool stuff.

Are you the
one with the

BIGGEST
HAIR,
Miss?

What do you think?

I'm also the

Poet Laureate.

Aotearoa New Zealand is the only country
in the world to give their poets laureate

toKotoKo:

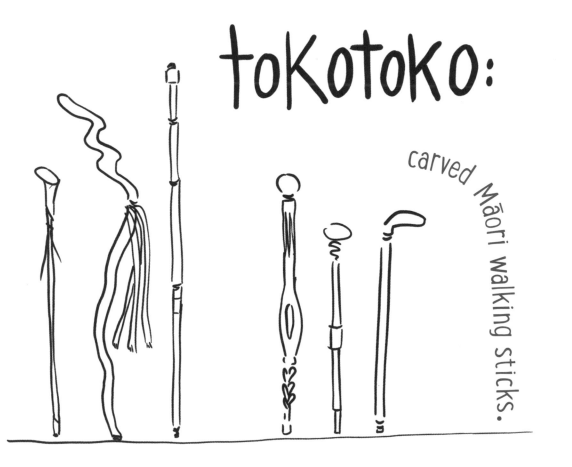

carved Māori walking sticks.

Poets give artist Jacob Scott special things
to carve into their own tokotoko.

I gave Jacob the fue.
When Samoan talking chiefs speak they
whisk the fue in the air to shoo away flies ...

real and imaginary ones.

When Jacob unveiled
his creation at the
Poet Laureate ceremony ...

I recognised an old friend.

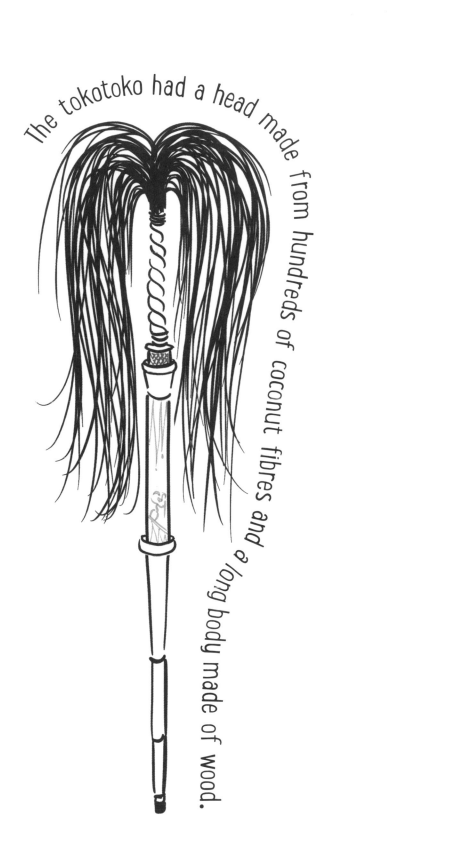

The tokotoko had a head made from hundreds of coconut fibres and a long body made of wood.

Everybody was amazed!

Sang

danced

laughed

prayed

We

chanted

drank

cried

recited

ate

After the celebration I brought my

tokotoko home to Waiheke Island.

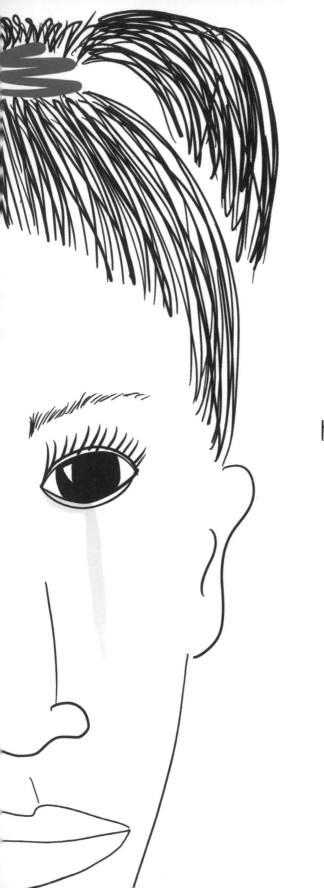

Puhi, the deckhand,
had been waiting for us.

She had tears in her
eyes when she saw
the tokotoko's beauty.

I began telling
its tale when —

Hahaaa!
Look at
that!

It was a boy.

I tried to ignore him
but he just got louder.

I turned to face the boy.

I was 10...

The end

Upu : Words

Ka pai, e hoa! Well done, friend! (Māori)

'Ofa atu Love to you (Tongan)

Kia manuia Best wishes (Rarotongan)

Malo lava Well done (Samoan)

Fakatalofa atu Thank you (Samoan)

Tui Atua Tupua Tamasese Tupuola Ta'isi Efi

A member of Samoa's royal line of chiefly families, former prime minister and head of state.

1st Pacific Women Poets & Their 1st Books

Konai Helu Thaman
You, the Choice of My Parents (1974)

Momoe Malietoa Von Reiche
Solaua, a Secret Embryo (1979)

Jully Makini
Civilized Girl (1981)

Grace Mera Molisa
Black Stone (1983)

Haunani-Kay Trask
Light in the Crevice Never Seen (1994)

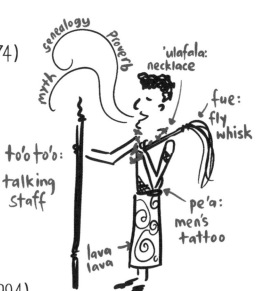

myth
genealogy
proverb
'ulafala: necklace
fue: fly whisk
to'o to'o: talking staff
pe'a: men's tattoo
lava lava

Fa'afetai & Thanks

Janet for bridging, Helen for clearing, Beate, Piggy Sue, Frodo (RIP) & Santana Farm, Sam (the poet), Sam (the publisher), Sam (the sister), Cinzia, Tusiata, PHIL, Sailau, Shenita, Rosina, Clive, Liz, Anne & St Jo's (Otahuhu), Vida, Sophia, Ben, Ari, Yukan, Sophie, Sepela, Davey, Javan for reading Mophead out *loud*!

Tino Wirihana & Matekino Lawless Kahui Whiritoi for MUKA, Caroline Tichborne & her roopu for weaving, Sarah my sherpa, Elise Fou Village & RLS' tomb for stones, E-Life Wild Turmeric & cuz Etu, Robin Peters for pounamu, Kathryn & NZ Book Council, Puhi for ♥, Matahiwi Marae, Tom & Jacob, Te Mata Winery Estate, John & Toby Buck, Peter, Chris & National Library, Dave, Micah, Auckland Uni for magical sabbatical, & Spike, who showed me I could draw & write.

First published 2019
Reprinted 2020, 2021
Auckland University Press
University of Auckland
Private Bag 92019
Auckland 1142
New Zealand
www.press.auckland.ac.nz

ISBN 978 1 86940 898 5

Published with the assistance of Creative New Zealand

A catalogue record for this book is available
from the National Library of New Zealand

Design by Vida and Luke Kelly Design

Printed by 1010 Printing International Ltd

For pictures on the back endpapers, thanks to the students
from St Joseph's School Otahuhu and Marlborough Boys' College;
to Tim Page for his photo of Selina (top, second to right);
to Florence Charvin for Poet Laureate portrait (bottom right);
to Penny Howard and Whitespace Contemporary Art for the painting
Dr. Selina Tusitala Marsh, 119 x 120 cm, acrylic on board, 2018 (top, third to right);
and to Picture Partnership/Andrew Dunsmore for photo of Selina greeting
HM The Queen at Westminster Abbey, London on Commonwealth Day 2016.

April 20th 2016   by lovey
Mommy you are as sweet
as honey and fill my heart
With it, you are made out of
Flowers thier for you are smelling
good for hours I am proud
to be your Youngest Son
Thats Why I have so much Fun.
Mum. you are Smart, Creative
So positive and all the above.
Mum does every Thig 4 Me.
She even rubs my knee.
Mum I Love you .....